The Boy in a Baseball Cap

戴棒球帽的男孩

Duo Er 朵而

translated by
Ouyang Yu 欧阳昱

PUNCHER & WATTMANN

Contents

Born in the 1970s in Shanghai, Duo Er, whose real name is Wu Yadi, is a member of the Shanghai Writers' Association and the Songjiang District Writers' Union. Her work has been widely published in such literary magazines as *Poetic Exploration*, *Chinese Poets*, *Shanghai Poets*, *Literary Weekly*, *Tide of Poetry*, *Flying Skywards*, *Yan Bian*, *Shandong Literature*, *Qingdao Literature*, *The World of Prose Poetry*, *Xinmin Evening* and *Literatures in Chinese*, and has been anthologized in such collections as *The Annual Collection of Poetry by the Poets Born in the 1970s in China* and *A Century of Selected Prose Poems*. She has published one collection of prose poems, *The Black Keys*, and has won a prize in the First Shanghai International Poetry Competition in 2016.

弄堂里戴棒球帽的男孩

他进来的时候还不怎么起眼
等到摘下棒球帽
露出半个脑袋时
几乎所有目光直接
被粘贴进了那面镜子

他安静地坐着
理发师在他下凹的头顶上洒水
窗外那棵梧桐
有一抹浅绿正在爬出来
弯弯的，很嫩

The Boy in a Baseball Cap in the Alleyway

When he came in, he was inconspicuous
When he removed his cap
Revealing half of his head
Nearly all the eyes were directly
Pasted onto that mirror

Quietly, he was sitting
A barber sprinkled water over the top of his concave head
Out of the Wutong-tree outside the window
A smear of light green was creeping out
Curved, tender

外科医生 Jame

进入家乐福不久
他就发现了
曾接受断掌移植手术的她

他决定过去打招呼：
嘿，珍妮
我是 Jame，还记得吗

或者这样：
珍妮
你的手现在怎么样

珍妮同时也认出他并急速冲过来：
Jame！
你看看给我做的是什么！

众目之下
黑皮肤的珍妮伸出了一只
白手掌

Surgeon 詹姆

Shortly after he got inside Carrefour
He found her
Who had had a palm transplant

He decided to go and say hello:
Hi, Jenny
I'm 詹姆 . You still remember me?

Or like this:
Jenny
How's your hand going?

At the same time, Jenny recognized him and rushed over:
詹姆 !
Look what you have done!

All eyes saw
The dark-skinned Jenny hold out
A white palm

一个男人的葬礼

牧师低声祷告着
在圣子圣灵中轻轻安放忧伤的人们
随白鸽步向墓地
棺木静静地在草地中央
等着感谢最后的恩赐

打着黑色领结的小男孩手持一朵野菊
他的童声湿润着整片墓地
"我要献给爸爸！"

看到此处，刚埋葬老父的朋友站了起来：
你看外国人的电影
就这么讲究

The Burial of a Man

The priest is praying, in a low voice
And people who have gently placed their sorrow amongst Son and Holy Spirit
Are walking towards the graveyard, following the white doves
The coffin, still, in the middle of the lawn
Waiting for the final blessings

A small boy, in a black bow tie, is holding a wild chrysanthemum
His voice moistening the whole graveyard
'I'll give this to my Dad!'

My friend, who has just buried his father, stood up:
You see, a foreign-made film
Is so sophisticated

丈夫

一个擅长沉默、喜欢回避敏感话题的男人
这一次在聚会上，直接藐视他那位
被冠以善良、真诚、有责任心的太太

他指着笑得正妖娆的太太：
"你敢揭露你的凶狠、残忍吗？
天哪！你一次次杀了我。"
他的声音几近哭泣

大厅瞬间寂静下来
他端着酒杯的手
一直在那摇晃

The Husband

A man, good with silence and at avoiding sensitive subjects
Directly looked down in this meeting
On his wife, known for her kindness, sincerity and responsibility

He pointed to his wife, smiling with an enchanting smile:
'Dare you expose your maliciousness and ruthlessness?
Heavens! You have killed me many times already'
His voice on the verge of tears

The great hall instantly went quiet
His hand, holding the glass of wine
Kept shaking

我们仨，还有那条河

大哥嘴馋
把偷吃光的水果罐头
往河里扔
村里小伙伴摸鱼时脚割伤了
我们就喊
阿盗三，你个天杀的

二哥愚笨
我掉进河里
他就坐在船尾发呆
看着我的头发渐渐失去踪影
当大人们轮流倒背溺水窒息的我时
他小声说
妹妹
死了

这次大哥回乡
沿着整齐的河坝走了一圈
见不到淤泥闻不到水草味
也没有遇到一个
相识的人

二哥依旧傻傻地
望向我
他说
河还在

The Three of Us, and the River

Big brother, a glutton
Ate up all the canned fruit
And chucked the cans into the river
When little mates in the village got their feet cut catching fish in the river
We'd yell:
You Goddamned Thief Three!

Second Brother was silly
When I fell into the river
He would sit on the stern, dazed
Watching my hair disappear, almost without a trace
When the adults took turns carrying me, nearly drowned
He would whisper, saying:
My sister is
Dead

When my big brother came back to the village last time
Taking a walk around the neat embankment
He did not see the mud nor could he smell the water grass
He had not even met anyone
He knew

Second brother still stupidly
Looked at me
Saying:
The river is still there

绿

竹笋冒尖时
石碑下有人小声说话
春来了
来了

满田野跑动的
不是穿着绿衣裳的娃
而是不再羞怯不管不顾的
油菜花

靠近土丘那片残垣还在
曾经有个丰盈少女向我招手
当时
风夺走了我眼睛

Green

Just as the bamboo shoots were sprouting
There was someone talking in a small voice underneath the gravestone, saying
Spring is coming
Coming

Running all over the field
Were not kids in green
But the canola flowers
That were reckless, no longer shy

The broken wall remained by the mound
Where once was a plump girl waving at me
It was just then
That a wind snatched my eyes off

教堂

靠近他需要穿过一排排长椅
阳光穿透六色玻璃
落在乐谱一样的睫毛上
有时也化作一只黑鸟绕着十字架飞

那个受难的人会抬起头
等待我
将身上所有的罪
加给他

The Church

To get close to him you need to go past rows of long benches
The sun, striking through the six-coloured glass
Falls on the sheet-music-like eyelashes
Sometimes turning into a blackbird that flies around the cross

The suffering one will raise his head
To wait for me
To put all my sin
On him

搭车人

乍看还以为是双女人手
捧着手机校对夜色
反光镜上几滴雨随街灯
有节奏地晃动
他额头、面颊以及举起的指甲便染上了
一种海蓝

这个浑身散发烟味酒味字味的男人
下车后发的图没有配上任何文字
忽然想起他居住的地方有个湖
每次和朋友去接他
窗户上贴着一颗头颅
被什么东西咬掉一块似的
露出湖的底色

Passenger in a car

At first glance, you thought it's a woman's hands
Cupping a mobile phone to proofread the colours of the night
On the rear-view mirror, drops of rain were swaying
Rhythmically with the streetlights
So that his forehead, his cheek and the raised fingernails were dyed
In a sea blue

This man, reeking with smells of cigarette, liquor and word
Posted the picture after he got out of the car, without any caption
On a sudden, I recalled there was a lake where he resided
Every time I fetch him with my friends
A head is glued to the window
Revealing the colours of the lake's bottom
Like something that had been bitten off

在荒芜里游弋

有风

月亮拔得很高
雀鸟将自己匿于树冠

他与夜并排躺着，眼内泛着点点清光
黑暗中划出一条河流
在虚实间迂回

夜又深了些
继水的清冷之后，乌鸦突然叫唤起来
他清瘦的身体便缓缓转过来，说
那是斑鸠

Cruising in the Wilderness

There was wind

The moon was pulled high
As the birds hid themselves in the crown of the trees

He was lying in parallel with the night, his eyes dotted with clear light
A river drawn out in the darkness
Meandering between the real and the virtual

Night, slightly deeper now
After the colding of the water, a black magpie suddenly called
His thin body slowly turning around as he said
That is a turtledove

他们

这条单行道直通嘉松路
两侧樱花正白
一排排冷杉
贴着风
压低鸟鸣

湖中央凉亭四个红檐角翘得很开
像一个舞者高高跃起
洒下火玫瑰
他摇头
认为那是鹤在寻找自己的羽毛

越过草坪许多声音突然凭空消失
庞大的静
打破着之前习惯了的一切
这种逆差在微妙中
彼此观察，衔接

眼前许多景可以制造扭力
咫尺之间扣着一种琢磨
不透的饱和
他终于把手合在另一个人手里
身体里那条暗流活了

Them

This single track went straight to Jiasong Road
Lined with the whitening cherry flowers
Rows of cold firs
Clinging to the wind
And lowering the birdsong

The cool pavilion, in the middle of the lake, with four widely open angles
Like a dancer that leapt high
And sprayed fiery roses
He was shaking his head
Thinking it was a crane looking for its own feathers

Many sounds that had crossed the lawn suddenly disappeared by themselves
An enormous stillness
Broke everything that one had grown used to
Such deficits, in the subtlety
Were observing each other, interconnected

Scenes before the eye could create a torque force
A mulling over the impenetrable saturation
Clasped in the closeness of it all
In the end, he merged his hand with that of the other
As the dark current in his body came alive

越过你

经历一些人事，每场变故
总有一些蛛丝可循
诸多细微是自身真切演绎
又硬生生遗落在那任其腐烂

一节松木也不过如此
几个符号站了出来，它们为前后衔接
相互拉扯、停顿
等候有人续上另一种可能
这更符合某条河流撕成碎片，又一次次
含恨合体

而越过这些，那个缓缓凝视
等待风干的人
他现在
什么都不剩了

Passing You

After experiencing events and people, each and every change
Has a spider's traces to follow
So many minutiae are deductions of their own real doing
They fall, stiffly, there, to let them rot

A piece of pinewood is no more than that
A few symbols stand out and, to be connected front to end, they
Stretch between themselves, and they pause
Waiting for someone to add to it another possibility
Which is fitting for a certain river to be torn into pieces and, again and again
Body-combined in hatred

But across all that, the one waiting to be wind-dried
Gave a slow gaze
He is left
With nothing now

断面

那个戴帽子吐圈圈的老克拉
拾起吉他
他唱颓废，仔细听
是一朵花打开又关闭
在一个盒子里尽情沙哑

在一墙黑胶唱片面前
没有人质疑自己正深陷一种深色主题
比如，手中这杯鸡尾酒是柜台那个小伙用深蓝火焰调制
她贴向桌面，微微颤着
一双褐色眼睛

贝斯依旧在几条线之间迂回
我也总是将他和她搞混
中场没有人离开
这晃荡夜
他唇边又吐出一个圈

A Section

The old colour, wearing a cap and blowing smoke rings

Picked up his guitar

He sang decadence, he listened carefully

It was a flower that opened and closed

Enjoying the hoarseness to the full, in a box

In front of a wall of black vinyl records

No one questioned if he was sinking deeply in a dark theme

An example: this glass of cocktail in hand was mixed by that boy with deep-

blue fire

She, leaning against the table, was shivering

A pair of brown eyes

Bass was circumvoluting between the lines

And I always confused him with her

In the middle of it all, no one left

On this rocking night

He spewed another ring around his lips

细月

声响小如符号
来时路上它们聚集，反转，裂变
细听，似飞虫走线忙于缝补夜的缝隙

从一个旧壳里挣脱，抵达另一个
似荣耀骨架间隐忍
重塑，等待后一次薄发

要说的话连同鳞片一起四散
地面又衍生一个个黑
攀附在亮处打结

我注意到这颗月亮
等不及流水，悄悄抹去的
是她自己

Thin Moon

Sounds like symbols
On my way, they gathered, turned around, fissioned
If you listen carefully, they were like flying insects, sewing the seams of the night

Breaking out of an old shell to reach another
Like a forbearance in the bone frame of glory
Re-shaping, waiting for a final thin burst

Words, to be spoken, disperse with the fish scales
Darkness, one after another, is derived from the earth
Tied in a knot, clinging to the lit spots

I note that the grain of moon
Quietly erased herself
Having no time, to wait for the flowing water

铅笔画

北海道最多的是
白与黑
山，街道，房屋，电线杆
凡是连接大地的
都与两种颜色有关

乌鸦不喜欢飞
彼此保持距离
穿过小镇
因为眼前一只乌鸦踩着同样节奏
你会发现所有笔画在推慢镜头

跟三浦相像的圭吾
在身后喊
ありがとう
他必是从店内小跑出来
又深深鞠着身的

A Pencil Drawing

In Hokkaido, there is a maximum
Whiteness and blackness
The hills, the streets, the houses, the telephone poles
Anything in connection with the land
Has something to do with the two colours

Magpies do not like flying
They keep a distance between themselves
And they go through a small town
Because a magpie treads the same rhythm
You find that all the drawn lines are in slow motion

Keigo, who looks like Miura
Is calling out behind me:
ありがとう
I'm sure he must be trotting out of the shop
With a deep bow

树下的人

阳光最辣时
直射树顶那些紫碎花
树荫下一圈最密阴影里
他感觉忧伤离哈姆雷特
又近了一步
自己中意的女人也急急赶来

她长什么样？这不重要
她拿了毛巾、剃须刀，提一壶清水
"来，刮一下"
一种从未有过的舒适传递周身
他甚至为喘不过气的脖子可以自由转动
忍不住嗯了一声

太阳继续往西走
留下成群苍蝇
除了嗡嗡煽动翅膀
这队刚解决饥渴的伞兵
满足地抬起头
凝视他

The Person under a tree

When the sun was at its most chili-hot
Striking down straight on the purple broken flowers
In the ring of the densest shades under the tree
He felt that his sadness was one step closer
To Hamlet
And the woman, after his own heart, was hurrying over

What did she look like? That's not important
She brought in a towel, a shaver and a kettle of clean water
'Come and I'll shave you'
A comfortableness, never experienced, travelled across his whole person
So much so that he thought that his breathless neck could turn around freely
He couldn't help uttering a sound of humph

The sun kept walking towards the west
Leaving swarms of flies
Except the buzzing, fluttering wings
The team of paratroopers, hunger just allayed
Raised their heads with satisfaction
And stared at him

穿

檬的父亲，经历过各种灾难
多次命悬一线，都一一捡了回来
唯独这一个字的病，折腾
捣鼓近两年，还没等新年钟声落定
由菩萨悄悄领走了

檬一身白，一根长麻布
从肩头一直往下绕，最后用一个结
锁在了腰眼
跟前些日子相比
他明显矮了一截

告别仪式结束后
寒风中走在前头的鲁南，突然停住脚步
双手捂在衣领处
他语速缓慢：
我把父亲穿在身上，已
好多年了

Wearing

Lemon's father has gone through all sorts of disasters
His life on the line on many an occasion, picked up and brought back, again
and again
Except for this one-character disease that *zheteng*ed
And *daogu*ed for nearly two years. But before the bell rang for the new year
He had been quietly led away by Buddha

Lemon, in full white, a long sheet of linen cloth
Fell down from his shoulders, ending up in a knot
At the eye of his waist
He was shorter
Than a few days ago

After the farewell ritual ended
Lu Nan, walking ahead in the cold wind, came to a sudden stop
His hands covering his collar
He spoke at a slow speed:
I have been wearing my father for
Many years

退潮后

风带走所有声源
海鸟凌空飞着
它们排列整齐
依次掠过礁石，沙滩，水面

分界处聚集着一股巨大寂静
当象牙白与之摩擦时
死去很久的海
醒了过来

After the receding of the tide

Wind had carried away all the sources of sound
Sea birds were flying in the air
In neat order
One by one across the reefs, the sands, the water

At the boundary was gathering an enormous quietness
When the ivory white was rubbing against it
The sea, long dead
Woke up

归

该上涨的水位
依然没动静
老皇历算准的时辰
原来并不是永恒不变的啊

有人开始嘀咕
另几个则始终保持静止状态
他们的影子比泥沙更粗粝
比贝壳更坚硬

涨潮啦
在夕阳沉重的淹没声中
几双赤脚突然明快起来，奔向
一条半露着身体的船

Return

The water level that ought to have risen
Remained motionless
The timing, accurately calculated according to the old royal calendar
Is not something that is eternally unchanging

Someone started muttering
The other few remained still
Their shadows rougher than the sands
And harder than the shells

Oh, the tide is rising!
In the heavy sound of drowning of the setting sun
Pairs of naked feet became abruptly brisk, rushing
Towards a boat, its body half exposed

回家

越往深处挺进
风浪更大
船只似要挣脱颠簸
箭一般，射出去

几个胆大男人冲在船头
他们奔跑，嗷嗷长叫
渐渐地，抽打船体的海浪声越来越密集
翻滚着势要吞没一切

船舱内，女人穿肠
而出的呕吐物中
死去很久的小鱼
突然哭了

Going home

The more one got in the depths
The greater the wind and the waves became
It looked as if the boat was about to break out of the heaving
Shooting, like an arrow

A number of men rushed to the bow
They were running, sending forth long shouts
Gradually, the waves that lashed the ship became more concentrated
Churning, endeavouring to swallow up everything

In the cabin, in the vomit
That came out of a woman's intestines
A small fish, long dead
Suddenly burst into tears

清明草

这些天不再阴冷
三月走后
有人开始将草磨成粉作引子
药膳房先生曾说消停不消停
春后即服

墓地回来
挂念容易生根
一些零碎光爬在蝴蝶身上
嫁接大片豌豆花
同时也往槐树弯曲了一个冬季的弧度里钻

梦里那个人
是喊着要见吗
先生没有作答
他顺手抓取的一把药膳
正一一别过

The Qingming Grass

Days are no longer dismally cold
When March walked away
Someone began grinding the grass into powder as a primer
The gentleman in the medicine shop said *xiaoting*, not *xiaoting*
Take it after spring

When one comes back from the graveyard
Missing is easy to strike roots
Fragmentary lights are creeping onto the butterflies
Grafting large spreads of pea flowers
And, meanwhile, boring into the curve that the ashes have been bending the
                                        whole winter

That person in the dream
Is he crying to meet
The gentleman did not respond
The handful of medicine he took, just like that
Was taking leave, one by one

又一次

夜落在寂静处
没有一件事可以转身说个明白

麻雀梳理羽毛为透亮的身份做着准备
风小心吹拂

你抛出的问题聚在月光抵达的地方
桉树没有回答

Once Again

Night fell where it was still
Not a single thing could turn around with an explanation

The sparrow was combing its feathers, in preparation for a transparent identity
And the wind was carefully blowing

The questions you chucked out were gathering where the moonlight had reached
But the gum had no answers

野百合

一层薄薄的还没落定的羽翼
需要轻轻安抚
它们斑斓，敏感
时而小颤

有人模仿你说话
突然大声喊一个人名
不，什么都没有
那些回音埋在山谷里很久了

The Wild Lily

A layer of feathers, thin, not yet dropped
that needed a gentle caress
gorgeous and sensitive, they
gave an occasional shiver

someone was mocking the way you spoke
suddenly calling out someone else's name
no, nothing happened
the echoes having been buried, for a long time, in the valley

你听

下雨了
雨水坠在屋顶、雨蓬、树丛
它们碰撞，谨慎而细碎
最终与地面合体
灌入耳的
是密集、尖锐

这里却在潜入另一种"静"
甚至连彼此呼吸的力气都被收纳了
或许因为眼前一对黑眼睛
而不是外面开遍的锋芒
这零度里挣脱出来的夜半
突然变得深谷

Listen

It was raining
the rain fell on the roofs, rain-canopies, clusters of trees
they were colliding with each other, careful and fragmentary
before they merged in one body with the earth
what poured into the ears
was density, sharpness

here, though, another kind of 'quietness' got in by stealth
so much so that the power to absorb each other's breathings was obtained
or perhaps because it was a pair of black eyes in the front
not the cutting edges widely open everywhere
the midnight that had struggled out of the zero degrees
suddenly turned into a deep valley

或者说

更像一种预知
一颗紧紧包裹自己的炎麦粒
在眼睑深处驻扎
这很像一颗白菜
土壤里汲取养分
某天被人轻巧地挤压、摘除
或用尖刀挑去根部
只提一颗头颅扔进滚滚沸水

正如你提过的，一些事要来
终有一些将离去
瞧这峭春寒，风到处欺凌
它们是成功的谎言家
用腌制白菜的方法一遍遍阉割
这片曾有我祖屋的土地啊
此刻除了黑，破败
它一望无际

Or

It's more like a precognition
an inflammatory grain, tightly wrapped up in itself
and took up its position in the depths of the eyelids
this looked very much like a bok choy
that took its nutrition from the soil
when someone someday, with a light touch, pressed it or removed it
or cut off its roots, with a sharp knife
hurtling its single head into the boiling water

just as you said, certain things will come
while other things may leave
look at this cold spring where the wind was everywhere bullying
a successful liar
castrating again and again, the way they pickled the bok choy
this land with my ancestral home, at this very moment
was boundless
except darkness and dilapidation

那年冬至

隔着一层白布
摸到她冰冷的手那么小
很想揭开遮盖她面部的白布
把脸贴上去
像小时候那样彼此摩擦
母亲走过来摁住我
她只允许我哭

这个让我含着她乳头睡去
养我长大的女人
如今躺在一块白布下
冰箱里杜冷定还有几支
要说的话还在肚子里热着
之前付出的一切
在死神面前毫无作用

被欺骗的绝望一层层涌来
压在胸口
我张大嘴用尽全部气力
冲破喉咙
呐喊
屋里除了父母兄嫂的哭泣声外
没有其他人的

At Winter Solstice that Year

Over a white cloth
you could feel that her cold hands were so tiny
you'd very much like to lift the white cloth covering her face
and put your face next to it
rubbing each other as you did when a child
when Mother came over and held me down
allowing me only to weep

this woman, who had brought me up
letting me sleep, with her tit in my mouth
was now lying underneath a white cloth
there were a few tubes of Dolantin in the fridge
and the words I wanted to say were still hot in my belly
what had been offered before
was of no use in front of death

despair, deceived, was surging, level after level
pressing down on the chest
I opened my mouth as wide as possible, yelling
breathing out of my throat
with all my strength
there was no one else in the house
except the tearful crying of my parents, my older brother and his wife

衣架

镜头留给我的
是他挂着的衣服里还有一件格子衫
那时
才隐约觉着什么是断背山

这里，牧场不怎么花哨
因为木窗上晾着一条粉色内裤
牵马路过的男孩将鼻孔彻底裸露在太阳底下

草地，牛马拍打着尾巴
一种枯败很久的花
突然满山红了起来

The Clothes Hanger

What the lens left me
was a checked shirt, underneath his garment hanging on the hanger
it was not till then
that I vaguely sensed what was a brokeback mountain

here, the pasture was not quite florid
because a pink knickers was sunning on the wooden window
a boy, who happened to pass by with a horse, thoroughly exposed his nose to
the sun

on the grassland, the cow and the horse were swishing their tails
a flower, withered for a long time
suddenly reddened a whole mountain

距离

还有什么不舍的
拥有海藻、金枪鱼的人
只需轻轻弹一节烟灰
余晖，潮汐，棕榈甚至风
都在点与点之间
选择一种弧线

海鸥停止叫唤
在两片烤熟的面包上
再轻轻抹上果酱
窗外那片小梅沙
有海
在死去

The Distance

What is there one doesn't want to give up on
all the one who owns the seaweed and the tuna
needs to do is to lightly tap off a section of cigarette-ash
the evening glow, the tide, the palm-trees and even the wind
are choosing a curve
amongst the dots

the seagull has stopped crying
jam is being gently spread
between the two slices of toasted bread
Xiaomeisha, outside the window
has a sea
that is dying

阿海郭

多年前在杭州
大伙就坐在类似城楼的亭子里
阿海郭突然站起来做了个假设
如果眼前所有灯火变成利箭或石块
向你砸来
会怎样

岁月一直在佐证人体各种机能的衰退
记忆的、听觉的、嗅觉的…
而杭州那个假设成了永不抹去的印记
其中二人回家途中被掉落的路牌砸到车上
一死一伤
另有一人去陕西收款途中被人丢在老车站
胸口插着一把剔骨刀

那个成天喊着说错话让雷劈的阿海郭
听说年前
剃度去了

Ah Hai Guo

Many years ago, in Hangzhou
we were all sitting in a pavilion that looked like a city tower
when Ah Hai Guo suddenly stood up and made a hypothesis
wondering what would happen when
all the lights in front of you were turning into arrows or stones
that were hurtled towards you

years were evidence of how various human functions had deteriorated
the mnemonic, the hearing, the smelling...
and the hypothesis in Hangzhou remained an unerasable mark
for a road sign fell smashing on the two of them on their way driving home
one dead and the other, injured
and a third, on his way to collect the debt in Shanxi, was thrown in the old
train station
a boning knife in his chest

and Ah Hai Guo who daily vowed that he'd get struck by thunder if he said
things wrong
had become a monk, his head shaven
early in the year

一个人的冬夜

那些消散的
终究无法还原真实
指间燃剩的烟灰，炙热过

圣洁，是迷离中夜包裹自己的
另一种白
比躯体更轻比昼夜更薄
有人相识又成陌路

梧桐过早凋谢
将所有伤痕弯成一个人的轮廓
而注视良久，我发现所有出处
都是一种假设

One Woman's Winter Night

Those that have become scattered
will never recover their truthful state
the remaining ashes between the fingers were once hot

holiness is another white
that wraps itself up at misty midnight
lighter than the body and thinner than the day or night
someone you meet that soon becomes a stranger again

the wutong tree has withered before its time
bending all the wounds into the silhouette of someone
after watching for a long time, I find that all the sources are
but a hypothesis

白衣人

那些夜晚，总是充满希望的

琵琶鱼伏在河面逗星星，吃水花
白衣人在芦苇丛中穿行
他们衣袂飘飘
缓缓招手

走亲戚的祖母驮着年幼的我往家赶，惦记着
床底下罐装结块的麦乳精是否被偷吃
患病的羊崽有没有站起来
似乎未曾察觉到面前发生的一切

直到那日，她一身素衣
在门口回头凝视
才记起那片芦苇是她种植的，那条河
她曾开挖过

Those in White

Those nights were always filled with hope

The anglerfish, in the river, were tickling the stars and eating the water flowers
while those in white were going through the reeds
their garments flying
and they were waving

grandmother, after visiting her relatives, carried me, a kid, on her back, and
                                        was hurrying home, wondering if
someone had stolen the caked malt extract from the tin underneath the bed
and if the sick lamb had stood up
and she didn't seem to be aware of anything that was happening before her

till that day when she, wearing white
stood at the door and turned to stare
it's not till then that she recalled that she had planted the reeds and had
dug the river

在喀什

所有的风景，仿佛为一个人而设
戈壁滩，胡杨，石头，鸟的翅膀
喀什，从深处散发的荒芜
至今没有一种色彩可以掩盖

在喀什，我终于把你一点点抹去
那座遥远城市，它只是
有伤的身体上一层厚痂而已

赶车的大爷挥手扬鞭，我也挥手
地面，几百道沟纷纷让路
它们像人的身体，又像是喀什的牛羊
在一种皱褶里急速晃动，留给喀什更深荒芜

在喀什那段时间
西北的风是往东边去的
有毒的种子不断撕裂着自己

荒芜上
一匹奔跑的烈马，呼哧呼哧
淌着血

At Kashgar

All the scenery seems set for one person
The Gobi Desert, the populus, the stones and the birdwings
Kashgar, a desolation that comes from the depths
And that refuses to be covered by any colours

At Kashgar, I have finally erased you, dot by dot
The distant city is but
A thick scab on a wounded body

The uncle, driving a cart, was whipping his whip as I waved my hand
And hundreds of gullies in the ground were making way
Resembling human bodies or the cattle or sheep in Kashgar
Rapidly swaying in a wrinkle, leaving more profound desolation in Kashgar

During that period of time in Kashgar
The wind went from the northwest to the east
And poisoned seeds kept tearing themselves

Over the desolation
A savage horse, running while puffing and blowing
Was bleeding

白枣树的日子

那时也热
一碗水泼出去，地面立马噗呲一声
短暂的湿之后，泥土又是泥土
未改变什么

屋后栀子花开了又谢
冷不防又冒出来一支更白的
蜜蜂吃饱了喜欢往土墙缝里钻
孩子们露出屁股在水塘里扑腾
岸上永远有个母亲撩了根长竹使劲追

最看不懂的就是西村文花家一棵白枣树
怎么摘也摘不完那些青白果
瞎眼的阿婆坐在院里
来人时假装一声一声咳
狗叫起来，鸡散开翅膀满地跑

从那个地方出来的人
有的走路很快，有的还在半路看风景
也有倒着走的，
前些日子遇到一个往回走的老同学
刚打声招呼，空气似的
一溜烟消失了

又快夏季，这天说变就变
轰隆隆几个响雷
开在头顶

Days of the White Jujube Tree

It was hot then
when a bowl of water was thrown, there was an instant hissing on the ground
after the momentary wetness, the mud remained the mud
and nothing had changed

the gardenias at the back of the house opened and withered
and, all of a sudden, something whiter came out
when the bees were fully fed, they liked to burrow into the seams of the earthen wall
kids, buttocks exposed, were splashing in the pond
always chased by a mother on the bank, with a long bamboo stick

it was hardest to understand the single white jujube tree, in Wenhua's
                                              house, in West Village
for you could never gather those endless green-white fruit
Grandma, blind, sitting in the courtyard
would pretend to cough when someone turned up
a dog barked and chickens, wings up, ran all around the place

people who came out of that place
walked very fast, a few would stop halfway to look at the scenery
and there were also those who would walk backwards
the other day when I met an old classmate who walked backwards
I greeted him but he disappeared
like the air

almost summer now and the day changed from the word go
a rambling thunder
overhead

查维拉

打翻龙舌兰的女人
更钟情于一支雪茄
这个烈日下披着斗篷、嗅觉灵敏的身体
因残缺而绝美

走入黑夜，她就是一把
危险狂妄的枪
酒吧里她用碎片式风暴，释放
男人的豪放与愤怒
女人的哭泣及颓废

与我而言，哥斯达黎加是陌生的
站在那更像沙漠中一棵树
她在树下哼着破败的歌
许多年后人们依然津津乐道于
她专属的龙舌兰、雪茄、还有
沙砾一般的嗓音

某个时段，我差点把她
当做我
身体的一部分

Chavilla

The woman who overturned the tequila
was more passionate about a cigar
the body, with a cape under the scorching sun and a keen sense of smell
was perfect because of its incompleteness

walking into the dark night, she was a
dangerous and arrogant gun
in a bar, she would give vent, in a fragmentary manner
to man's extravagance and fury
and women's weeping and decadence

for me, though, Costa Rica was strange
she stood there, more like a tree in a desert
she stood under the tree, singing a broken song
but, years after, people still talked about
her tequila, her cigars and
her sandy voice

at one stage, I almost regarded her
as part
of my own life

残荷

与身后那片茂盛不同
池塘正中立着一株残荷
我看到另一段生命在褐色深处游离
莲蓬似断非断
这种悬着的空
与养了多年习惯奔跑着回家的羊只
被杀时
眼睛弥散着半开半合
比起来
如出一辙

What Remained of a Lotus-flower

Different than the lushness behind it

what remained of a lotus-flower stood right in the middle of a pond

I saw a section of life dissociate itself in the depths of brownness

the seedpod of the lotus was half-broken

such hanging-looseness

resembled the way

a sheep that had grown used to running home

over the years

kept its eyes half open

when killed

爱，安静久了就是蓝

这里没有咆哮
一如你轻轻引用经典
提前温润誓言

荒芜偷偷发芽，你悄悄说话
与所有亮过的星星一般，为了留下
身后那些路标，关键词销声匿迹

当孤独强大到极致
身体某处你细腻过的蝴蝶效应
无人临摹

我安静下来，用你叮嘱的方式
活着
在另一种蓝里

Love; It was Blue When Quiet for Long

There was no roaring here
the way you quoted a classic, gently
warming up your pledge, ahead of time

desolation sprouted by stealth, and you talked, quietly
like all the stars that had sparkled, in order to keep
the road signs behind you when keywords vanished

when solitude was so strong that it went extreme
the butterfly effect somewhere on your body that you had subtled
defied copying

I grew quiet and lived
the way you urged
in another blue

叶子

光透过玻璃弹射到膝盖
受伤部位似乎也跟着跳了下
那片杏黄还在树上挂着
偶尔有风贴过去
躲闪变得无足轻重
像一个被废弃符号

如果有个人在一片即将凋零的叶子面前
跟你说话
耳根会慢慢发炎
那些话终究因腐烂脱离原有躯体
这很像另一种破败
却尽力缓慢，极致

接着，它真的掉了下去
现在这棵树什么也没有了
我注意了很久
直到护士针尖似的声音飘进：
来，量体温了

The Leaf

The light, through the glass, leapt onto the knees
and, along with it, the injured part seemed to have also leapt
the patch of apricot yellow was still hanging on the tree
occasionally, when the wind got close
hiding was of no significance
like a sign, cast aside

if someone spoke to you
before a leaf, about to wither
the roots of the ears might become inflammatory
those words might eventually detach themselves from the original body, for
reasons of decay
this was like another kind of ruin
although it tried to be slow, to be extreme

then, it fell, for real
now, the tree had got nothing on it
I had been paying attention for a long time
till the nurse's voice, like the point of a needle, came drifting in:
Come and take your temperature

哭灵人

她双手掩面
把头伏向灵柩
这个嚎啕声中一口一个亲娘的女人
这个紧闭双眼泪水流淌的女人
这个没穿孝服头发凌乱满脸皱纹的女人
比那几个跪在地上磕头的儿子媳妇都显眼
赴丧者侧耳听她哭了些啥
很多人因那嚎啕悲戚声动容
开始念叨死者生前种种的好
有人落泪也有人拭泪

不一会唢呐铜钹响起
她站起来端起一碗水咕隆隆灌下喉
继而朝领头的道士喊：
差不多了，赶
下一家

The One Who Was Crying Before the Bier

Hands covering her face
she put her head on the bier
the woman who kept saying 'Mother' in her wailing
the woman with tears running out of her closed eyes
the woman, not in mourning, with dishevelled hair and a face of wrinkles
was more conspicuous than the sons and daughters-in-law, on their knees
and kowtowing
the attendees, their ears pricked up, were trying to listen
many, moved by her sad wailings
began talking about the kindnesses of the dead
some was dropping his tears and others were wiping off theirs

when the suona horns and brass cymbals were sounded
she stood up and drank noisily from a raised bowl
before the monk, at the head of the procession, yelled:
Time to go and let's hurry
To the next family!

塘口

水葫芦泛着热气簇拥在一起
借助光将自己投射在人脸上
折成风

不敢抬头仰望天空
害怕云朵离去，令这条江只剩下一副骨架
从此你便有了忧伤理由与我冷对

长时间横渡之后
船桨开始在褪变的白上
撕裂水的声音

At the Mouth of the Pond

Water hyacinths were huddling together
and, with the reflected light, they projected themselves onto the human faces
bending them into wind

one didn't dare raise one's head towards the sky
in fear of the clouds leaving   the river to only a skeleton
after that, you have reason to be sad and to treat me coldly

after spending a long time crossing the river
the oar began on the fading white
sound of the tearing water

我在更年期

说这话的是老钱
这个五十多岁身高一米八八
听说在新疆又一下就能蹿高 4 厘米的男人
一个月前气跑了助理
一周前为不转的轴承与人打赌用力砸了手掌
就在半小时前他宣称自己要撞墙给大伙看

被劝回办公室后
冷静许多，开始吐露一点心事
预约了后天要去做打鼾症检查
跟儿子明天彻底摊牌不接受他那个女朋友

他站起神情色越发沮丧
你说我这个病
是否被家里那个婆娘
给传染了

It's My Year of Change

It was Lao Qian who said that
this man, 50 years of age and standing at 1.88 meters
allegedly could jump to a height of 4 cm in Xinjiang
made his assistant so angry that she ran away a month ago
smashed his palm when laying a bet about the gearing that was not turning
a week ago
and announced half an hour ago that he would show how he could hit
against a wall

after he was talked back into the office
he calmed down and began revealing
that he had an appointment about his sleep apnea the day after tomorrow
and would lay all his cards on the table tomorrow to his son that he would in
no way accept his girlfriend

when he rose, he looked even more dejected
wondering if his condition
had been a result
of infection
by his wife at home

漂流瓶

往身体里填沙
满了满了
驻岸的鸟冲向渔火
眼前这条河，一再收纳余音
轻轻翻过来世

看不到浮生，夜便是漂流瓶
鱼结对吸出彼此的毒汁
云继续游，直至
另一种枯竭
说到这
你哭了很久

A Drifting Bottle

Filling the body with sands
to brimful
the birds, stationed on the bank, were rushing towards the fishing fire
the river, before the eye, kept receiving the remaining sound
gently turning the next life over

when you can't see the floating life, night is a drifting bottle
the fish, in pairs, suck the poisonous liquid out of each other
the cloud keeps drifting till
another kind of drying up
talking about that
you cried, for a long time

看得见的声音

从一种辨识度上获取的密码，轻盈而讨巧，
像善变的唇，一边是爱在作祟，
另一边有黑暗佐证的痕迹。

在一种卷曲上舒展，听力惧怕寂静，
为一坛酒痴醉的人，未必走失抑扬顿挫
旦角远去的背影，是念想在纯粹中挺身而出。

由一种跳跃带动山水，远古近在咫尺，
体内涌动的热是一个个符号，即便驾驭着它们，
也无法解释忧伤为何无时不刻相随。

又一颗陨落的星，击中一种柔软，
波及的壮阔在一种蓝里渗透，
我看到光年轻而澎湃，漫步而来。

天空中，布满河流的声音。

The Visible Sound

Code, when obtained via recognizability, is light and clever
like a changeable lip, love at work on one side
and, on the other, traces of darkness in evidence

spreading over a curl when hearing is afraid of stillness
the one, intoxicated with a pot of liquor, may not necessarily lose the cadences
the departing back of a dan actor is the mind-thought that comes forward

with a leap that moves mountains and waters, far ancient times are within reach
the heat, surging in the body, is but signs, and even if you can ride them
you can't explain why sorrow follows all the time

another fallen star hits the soft spot
the vastness that the waves reach is pervading inside a blue
when I can see light that is young and turbulent, coming in pervasive steps

the sky, full of the sound of the river

夜无根

不为人知的夜，疼惜着自己
一寸一寸长成荒草

我甚至忘了饥饿羊只，投来人一样的眼睛
那个山坡已然找不到一颗草籽

在冷水里打捞自己活着的样子
我听见浮萍，一直在喊疼

Rootless Night

The night, unknown, pities itself
growing weeds, inch by inch

I've even forgotten the hungry sheep, whose eyes are human like
not a single seed of grass is now findable on the slope

salvaging, in the cold water, the way I lived
I heard the duckweed, crying in pain

夜，落在最轻处

是的
贴着身体投射在墙上，风就在窗口
藤蔓，青瓷，老式打字机
与行距一起错落有致

有人抱着书抬手看表，又探头看雨
对于时间，黑暗中秒针最具权威
既无法给出一个确切答复，唯有将似有似无
演绎到极致
这多少令翻阅声，变得更轻
风在窗口，也很轻

来之前是小雨，从几滴到稍密
再到此刻的稀疏
如匍匐在一块白色遮雨布上的黑夜
失声痛哭

Night, Fallen where It Was the Lightest

Yes

sticking on the body and projected on the wall, the wind was right at the
mouth of the window

the vines, the china and the old typewriter

were well-proportioned with the line spacing

someone, holding a book, raised his hand to look at his watch, then he held
out his head to see the rain

about the time, the second hand in the darkness was most authoritative

though not able to give a definite answer, it could play the half-have

in the extreme

which somehow made the page-turning lighter

the wind at the mouth of the window was also light

before the arrival, it was a small rain, from a few drops to slightly dense

till sparseness now

like the darkness lying prostrate over a white rain cloth

bursting into tears

有种伤痛还存在体内

我总是听到风铃小声摇响自己
然后看到雨落下来
它落下来的样子像极了一种悲哀
小小的，不让人察觉

我惊讶于那些紧紧护住忧伤的尘埃
为了不让风掠夺
它们
一次次掩埋自己

There is Pain that Remains inside the Body

I always hear wind chimes shake themselves, making a small noise
then I see the rain fall
in a way that quite resembles a sadness
tiny, refusing to be noticed

I'm amazed by the dusts that closely protect the sorrow
to stop the wind from plundering
they
bury themselves, again and again

陌生人

那天迷路后
跟一个路人
搭讪

他亲切温善
问我怎么不小心
把自己弄丢呢

他很干净
什么也没有
赤条条的

The Stranger

The other day when he lost his way
he accosted
a passer-by

he was nice and kind
saying: Why am I so careless
as to have lost myself?

he was clean
he got nothing on
he was very naked

存在

她点烟，继续要一杯咖啡
懒散的人喜欢把身体往沙发更深处挪
似要把耗费了大半光景的自己
不留痕迹地埋葬掉
只留一小截陌生的，慢慢养着

靠近阳台位置
一个有胡须的男人几次看过来
镜片后，那是一张被撕成碎片又粘合的脸
她突然落泪
说看到了他前半生

Existence

She lit a cigarette and wanted another coffee
this lazy person wanted to move herself deeper in the sofa
as if intending to bury herself without a trace
who had spent more than half of her life
keeping only a short, strange section, to raise, slowly

on a seat near the balcony
a man with moustache looked her way a few times
behind his glasses was a face stuck together after being shredded
she, all of a sudden, was shedding tears
saying that she had seen the first part of his life

深处的声音

以为听见寂静的声音
看到花开，便是好的
聆听雨后聚集的细微声，才发现
这些年太多藤蔓需要梳理
深藏于枝节末端，且一次次
打开身体又颓谢的
早就不是单个的花蕊了

耳边，又时不时出现另外一种声音
跳跃着前行，像一只蝴蝶的呼喊
又像是雨滴落在瓦片上
弹出的那种浑圆
它们从圆润滑向静默
最后渐渐消失在更空寂处

没有刻意去想你走了多久
每次流浪猫回头，我发现你的眼睛
长在它们身上，对着我
目光冷峻

我能忍住的，是一声叹息

另一头，蔷薇花开了

Sound from the Depths

One assumes that it is good
to hear the sound of silence and to see the flowers open
it is not till after listening to the gathered minutiae of the rain that one found
that many a vine, over the years, required sorting out
as they were hidden deeply among the ends of the branches and opened,

again and again

the flowers that were again withered
and that were not single a long time ago

in my ears, occasionally, another voice
went jumping forward, like the cry of a butterfly
or the roundness played
by the fall of raindrops on the tiles
as they slipped from roundness to silence
disappearing, gradually, into more emptiness

I didn't purposefully wonder how long you had gone for
every time the stray cats turned their heads, I found your eyes
on them, turning towards me
with cold eyes

all I could stand was a sigh

on the other side, rose flowers were opened

面包圈有秘密的鸟鸣

她的脸被一部分果酱遮盖
羽毛，忧伤在滋长
天空，像祖母染过的卡其布
斑斓之外呈现一种均匀
天空，有时又像椰汁
将疼痛的味蕾
一次次留白

窗外这只蝴蝶，没有因雨的冰凉而退却
它沉重的翅膀下挟带着
另一个人的困顿
隐约中还有鸟鸣未绝

之后，长时间沉默的人
将颓废的秘密
塞进面包圈

There Were Secret Birdsongs inside the Doughnut

Her face was covered by part of the jam
the feather, sadness growing
the sky, like the khaki dyed by Grandma
presenting an evenness beyond the gorgeousness
the sky, sometimes like the coconut juice
providing blank spacing, again and again
for the tastebuds of pain

the butterfly outside the window did not back off because of the icy rain
its heavy wings carrying
the exhaustion of someone else
and there was unended birdcall that was faint

subsequently, the one who had been silent for a long time
stuffed his decadent secret
inside the doughnut

九娟

那年秧苗刚插上
九娟在田埂上哭喊着疯跑
风一阵阵压过来又忙不迭
收回去

咬住九娟小腿肚的土灰蛇
连同呼呼风声缠绕在一起
垄沟里水凉着，天空
飞得很低

离开家乡后再没见过九娟
有人说她嫁给一个渔夫
四十岁后水产生意发迹
赚来的全给一个小年轻骗走了

前些日子，在普陀山擦肩而过的几个尼姑中
有个特别像九娟
连喊了几声
都没应答

Jiujuan

That year, when the rice seedlings were just planted
Jiujuan cried as she ran wildly on the ridge of the rice paddy
the wind pressed down, in ripples, before it hurriedly
retrieved itself

a grey earth snake that wound itself around her leg
entangled itself, too, with the noisy wind
the water was cooling in the furrow while the sky
was flying low

after I left home I have never seen Jiujuan again
some said she had married a fisherman
when she made a fortune in aquatic business after 40
she lost all her earnings to a young swindler

a few days ago, among a number of nuns that I went past at Putuo Mountain
there was one who looked particularly like Jiujuan
I called her a few times
but she didn't make a response

红棉鞋在场记手里

站在左侧的是韩导
摄影师在另一侧
为拍摄特写
两人争得面红耳赤
而脚底下这个女人，头发散在床中央
大腿压住半条被褥

两人争论激烈
眼睛就没往那处瞅
一个说找准位置
另一个说还是需要点表情才行

躺在那时间久了
觉得冷
她顺势把被褥盖上了
这时他们口径一致
ACTION

The Red Cotton Shoes in the Hands of the Clapper Boy

Standing on the left was Director Han
and the cameraman was standing on the other side
they were arguing, red in the face
about how to shoot a close-up
and the woman at their feet had her hair spread about in the middle of a bed
her thigh over half a quilt

they two were so fiercely arguing
they didn't even look
one said one should find the actual spot
and the other sad that more expression was needed

lying there for quite some time
she felt cold
so she pulled the quilt over herself
when they came to an agreement:
ACTION

下月光

她体内藏着一条河流
湍急时和他躺一起，慢慢渗透
将他变为森林
这是长时间禁锢欲望后该有的样子
从荒凉到宽宥

夜爬过来，覆盖白杨
覆盖鸟的羽毛
覆盖湖面
那块被流言灼伤的天空
看不到了

月亮游出她身体
清冷冷的
还需要一点灰蒙，慢慢养着
远看，她
更像一株枯芙

Moonlight Down

She had a river hidden inside her body
she lay alongside him when it became turbulent, slowly seeping
turning him into a forest
a situation that ought to be after a long time of imprisoned desire
from desolation to forgiveness

the night was creeping over, covering the poplars
covering the birds' wings
covering the face of the lake
till the sky, scorched by gossip
became invisible

the moon swam out of her body
clean and cold
a little more fuzziness was needed, to be kept slowly
if looked at from a distance, she
was more like a withered hibiscus

黑光

更多时候我蜷缩在影子里
这安全的，没有人顾及的影子
此刻和我紧紧相拥
我们有着一样的肺泡
长在月光背面
任由暗处那条没有汽笛的河流
一次次划来又一次次划走
我们咬紧嘴唇
绝不发出一条鱼断裂翅膀的声音

更多时候我把你名字从一段残光里啄去
又一道黑的口子
长在影子深处
那片该有雨水的地方
有紧闭的眼睛
里面滚动的还温润着
始终没有落下
它在影子里奔跑
找一个对饮的人

Black Light

More often than not, I curled into my own shadow
the safe shadow that no one paid any attention to
was now holding me in a tight hug
we had similar alveolus
grown on the back of the moon
letting, at will, the whistle-less river
come rowing in and going rowing away
we bit our lips
refusing to make the sound of a fish with broken wings

more often than not, I pecked at your name, taking it from a remnant light
another black cut
grown in the depths of the shadow
in the place where there should be rainwater
there were closed eyes
what was rolling inside was still warm
never falling
it ran inside the shadow
in search of someone to drink face to face with

靠近海与山谷

乌云已无声翻滚一会了
榆树林那一片最厚重
灰色中央带一股浓郁的褐
几声闷雷
天空像张开大嘴的牛蛙
突兀着径直往上跳

大雨前挖出不少土豆，连根躺在地面上
被打开的、松软的碎泥
几条细长小虫缠绕在一起
又一声雷响在头顶
雨在云层里密谋
一场战争

说闽南话的阿灿婆，粗嗓门
嘴一瘪，霍罗罗几下
粉嫩肥小猪穿过她裤腿，排队跑进猪圈
鸭子去了池塘，黑狗躲在水泥板下
大雨炸开锅似的，迅猛有力
正在孵蛋的鸡急急叫起来

那个夜晚
雷响了很久
我们没有说话，只静静听着
海一样
天黑沉沉的，没有
褪去

Near the Sea and the Valley

Dark clouds had been rolling for a while now
they were at their heaviest and thickest over the elm forest
the greyness carried in it a rich brown
a few peals of thunder
when the sky resembled a gaping bullfrog
that leapt straight, abruptly

quite a few potatoes were dug out before the big rain, lying on the ground, with roots
in the opened-up mud, soft and fragmented
a number of long worms were entangled
another thunder overhead
the rain was plotting in the clouds
for a war

Aunty Ah Can who spoke Manlam ngy, in a loud voice
'clucked' a few times, her mouth flattened
when little pink fat piggies went right past her trousers, in a line, into the sty
ducks had gone to the pond while the black dog was hiding itself underneath
                                                    the concrete slab
a big rain, in a sound of deep-frying, came quick and violent
the hen laying an egg called out hurriedly

that night
the thunder was loud for long
we didn't say anything, just listening, quietly
like an ocean
the sky was overwhelmingly dark, not
receding